My Free Gift to You

Discover How to Get Rid of Stress & Anxiety and Reach Inner Peace in 20 Days or Less!

To help speed up your personal transformation, I have prepared a special gift for you!

Download my full, 120 page e-book "Mindfulness Based Stress and Anxiety Management Tools" (Value: $9.99) for free.

Moreover, by becoming my subscriber, you will be the first one to get my new books for only $0.99, during their short two day promotional launch. I passionately write about: social dynamics, career, Neuro-Linguistic Programming, goal achieving, positive psychology and philosophy, life hacking, meditation and becoming the most awesome version of yourself. Additionally, once a week I will send you insightful tips and <u>free e-book offers</u> to keep you on track on your journey to becoming the best you!

That's my way of saying "thank you" to my new and established readers and helping you grow. I hate spam and e-mails that come too frequently – <u>you will never receive more than one email a week! Guaranteed.</u>

Just follow this link:

<u>tinyurl.com/mindfulnessgift</u>

Please be aware that every e-book and "short read" I publish is written truly by me, with thoroughly researched content 100% of the time. Unfortunately, there's a huge number of low quality, cheaply outsourced spam titles on Kindle non-fiction market these days, created by various Internet marketing companies. I don't tolerate these books. I want to provide you with high quality, so <u>if you think that one of my books/short reads can be improved anyhow, please contact me at:</u>

<u>contact@mindfulnessforsuccess.com</u>

<u>I will be very happy to hear from you, because that's who I write my books for!</u>

Introduction: Why Meditation for Life Success?

Looking to be happy . . . not just fake smiles anymore? Sick of being held up and helpless, a victim of terrible circumstance? Do you really want to be a slave to your emotions anymore?

Do you ever wonder how some people are able to seemingly control their emotions?

Are you so depressed and negative that no one really enjoys spending time with you? Well, I was not necessarily talking to you, but if it speaks to you, you have picked up the right book! The above questions were the very ones that I asked myself before delving into meditation. It was not the first time I had engaged in such self-questioning, but it was the LAST!

In this book I share with you how my life was stifled by stress, worry, depression and guilt. I was going nowhere in a hurry and having a miserable time. Life was a chore and I was miserable. I never slept, was constantly stressed, and a hot mess, until the day I really actually began to understand meditation and put it to work for me!

There are techniques to step out of your thinking and allow your mind to rest. Also included are methods that will allow you to see your thoughts and fears for what they really are: not REAL. You will be able to successfully take a step back mentally and observe what is really going on in that brain of yours. I give you the gift of peace that I was able to attain through present moment awareness. Talk about the gift that keeps on giving! You will learn how to be peaceful and okay, even joyful, in each and every moment you are living! Have you seen those people walking around, truly content? That is what I am going to share with you.

Once you are unchained from the shackles of fear, doubt and worry, you will be able to finally achieve your goals step by step. You will unlock the self-confidence that has always been inside of you. That's right, self-confidence will come from YOU, and not what others may think or feel about you . . . hence the "*self*" part!

You are beginning a new chapter in your life by simply purchasing this book. Be excited! It is unlike anything you may have tried before. No more searching for the newest self-help program/life coach or the latest self-help book to hit the NY Times' bestseller list. Your search for the greatest therapist who will walk you through life is over. You will be in control of your life, your reactions, and your joy! You will finally be able to achieve success and holistic well-being. You are ready!

Thanks again for buying this book, I hope you enjoy it!

Chapter 1: Meditation? What it's all about?

"The gift of learning to meditate is the greatest gift you can give yourself in this lifetime"

Sogyal Rinpoche

I was always under the assumption that meditation was about clearing your mind; that it was the absence of thought. I thought that it was only for monks on a mountain top. Exclusively for Yoga masters in white sheets saying, "ommmmm," while sitting cross-legged. In all actuality, meditation is simply stepping outside the thought process. It is not the *absence* of thought but the *awareness* of thought. When meditating, you take a step back from actively thinking your thoughts, and instead see them for what they are. The reason why meditation is helpful in reducing stress and attaining peace in my life is that it gives my over-active consciousness a break. It is a mental time out. Just as the body needs rest, so does the brain. I was running mine ragged, burning out, thinking thoughts and "feeling emotions" that were not even *real*. Taking the time to meditate helps me to retain control over myself, the one thing in life I *can* control.

I was constantly fighting everything going on in my life, with my mind. Not just active battling, but worrying too. I was not able to accept things going on in my life; from the way my relationships with the opposite sex were going, how my job performance was being

Meditation has been around for thousands of years. It is used religiously and spiritually by many people all over the world. It is also used by people who are not spiritual at all. It has practical applications in reducing stress and increasing mental clarity that are useful to anyone. Calm your mind and give your conscious a "time out."

Stress in the mind has an effect on the body because it causes us to physically be in a "survival mode." This can cause serious physical problems over time because we were not designed to function in fight or flight mode on an everyday basis. Sure it is helpful when running from a saber-toothed tiger or when fighting on the frontlines, but when experienced every day, the physical effects are pestilent. Stress kicks in our immune system as well, and having an overworked immune system is never a good idea. Here is a list of only ten of the many health problems caused by stress:

1. Hypertension that can lead to heart attacks or death
2. Joint/muscle/back pain
3. Headaches
4. Gastrointestinal issues
5. Asthma/allergies
6. Alzheimer's Disease
7. Fatigue and sleep problems
8. Obesity (which causes its own wide range of health issues) or eating disorders

9. Frequent infections and colds

10. Rashes and other skin problems

Meditation will not only improve your physical health, but your emotional and mental health as well. How can something that sounds so easy help in so many areas of your life? Well, I will tell you that meditation is not *easy,* but simplistic in nature. It takes practice and focus, but there is not much to it when you break it down. It is a simple process (or set of processes to choose from).

Meditation does not have to be complex at all. Do you need candles, Zen music, or chanting? Well, you can utilize these things, but it is not necessary. Meditation can be done while walking. It can be done while lying or sitting in a cool, quiet place. As you get better at it you may be able to do it anywhere, at any time. You do not need to set aside hours to meditate (although that might be nice); minutes a day will show you results.

The options are extensive and it is all about you and what works for you. What allows you to take a mental step back? What allows you to put your mind on auto pilot, pause your thoughts and lets you take a moment in the passenger's seat?

In short time frames, with practice, I was able to find clarity, focus, and the ability to be calm. I had never felt better. I began sleeping longer and more deeply. That elephant no longer took a seat on my chest for hours on end.

Meditation can provide what you need to better yourself: a sense of calm. This newfound peace provides health benefits, such as better sleep, loss of excessive body weight or healthy gain of muscle and lower blood pressure. It also actually improves brain function. A calm and strong brain can be the surefire path to accomplishing your goals. I speak not only of improvement in your work, but improvement in yourself as a person. When you become a more peaceful person, your personal relationships will see much improvement.

My intimate relationships are no longer consumed by my stress and over-thinking. My friendships are much more fulfilling. I am not a pain to be around anymore, and I do not worry about being a burden to others. I feel fulfilled in my life now and am actually *happy*. Who doesn't want to be around a happy person? From business dealings to more intimate relationships, I am a calmer person. Who would not find that appealing and magnetic?

You deserve a pat on the back for taking your first step in ultimately changing your life for the better; for your benefit, and the benefit of those around you. Many people just wander through life and wonder, "why me?" You should be congratulated. It is a leap, and not many are even willing to take a chance on it. What do you have to lose? Nothing. You have everything to gain!

Chapter 2: Let's Get Started! Various types of Meditation

There are many different types of meditation. Some of them will help you gain a boost in your dragging immune system, others will help you reduce stress in your life, and show how to run your emotions instead of allowing them to run you. You can choose from a variety of different techniques that will allow you to improve all areas of your life.

Our brains and bodies are designed in a way that when they are exposed to stress, the prefrontal cortex (the part of the brain that makes decisions, regulates productivity, attention and emotion) shuts down and is overruled by the lower brain (where instinct takes over). For the short term, our bodies were designed to work this way for good reason, and after the threat is gone the prefrontal cortex takes back over. Yet, when a person is under stress for long periods of time, this does not always happen. A plane cannot be flown on autopilot forever. There is a malfunction in regaining control. Meditation can help with this.

Personally, I felt out of control. I felt that I could not control over my emotions such as sadness and anger. I could never control my attentiveness or keep my focus for very long. This was a long, ongoing struggle for me. From high school through my mid 20s - I was a mental mess. When one is a mental mess, it is difficult to perceive and regulate emotion. I just wanted to be happy, and most of all I wanted to be successful in running my own business.

I was deeply depressed every day. I was always over-emotional or worried to the point of being petrified to make any decision AT ALL. Even figuring out what to eat was torture, let alone deciding what to do next to progress my life.

I failed in my career as a HR consultant at a large firm because I simply could not concentrate. I would either be too bummed out to be productive, or doubted myself so much that I stifled my own career. I tried opening my own business as a freelance consultant, but sadly enough, I would up distracted by anything (TV, internet, or the dust bunnies on the floor). I was unmotivated, depressed, and wondering why bad things always happened to me.

After I learned to meditate successfully (it does take practice), I was able to get my brain back in order, or rather, just in order. During this process my emotions and my health fell back in line. I was healthier and happier. I was focused and was able to gain momentum in all areas of my life. Instead of the chain reaction of terrible events happening to me, my life was snowballing in a direction that I liked. One thing leads to another, and this time I was enjoying every minute of it. I was finally in control of my emotions, my attention, my*self*.

As I have continued to study and research about meditation, I have discovered various scientific proofs of its benefit to the body. In fact, a Harvard Medical School study suggests that the continuous practice of meditation has a positive effect on the genes and brain activity of chronically stressed people. John Denninger, a scientist/psychiatrist from Harvard Medical School, who is also director of research at the Benson-Henry Institute for Mind Body Medicine at Massachusetts General Hospital, completed studies showing that being in a meditative state can activate and deactivate certain genes that relate to the body's stress resistance and immune system functions. Denninger said that there is a true biological effect with regular practice of meditation and it can benefit the whole body, not just the brain.

Denninger also asserted that research on the positive effects of breath management and "inhabiting the present moment" to a person's overall health and wellbeing is absolutely important, and needed further studying. His most recent research, set to conclude in 2015, refers to about 210 chronically stressed individuals that he and his team divided into three groups. Participants had each undergone extremely high levels of stress for the past six months.

The first 70 were made to practice Kundalini, a fast-paced style of Yoga. The next set of 70 was allowed to do traditional meditation techniques, such as deep breathing and guided meditation, while the last group listened to audio books that talked about stress relief. The participants practiced their technique for 20 minutes a day in their own homes and private spaces.

Different from his other earlier experiments, this experiment was the first time his team included highly stressed people as subjects. Initial results gave them positive findings. They found that meditation increased the metabolism of energy and secretion of insulin among all participants, and it also lessened their response to inflammation and stress.

A 2012 study[1] by scientists from the University of California at Los Angeles, headed by Nobel Prize winner Elizabeth Blackburn, revealed that an intensive 12-minute daily Yoga meditation practice for two months can boost telomerase action by about 43%. This means that meditation can slow down physical aging caused by chronic stress. Telomerase is a body enzyme that adds DNA sequence repeats to the body. It is also called the "immortality enzymes."

Decision-making became easier and easier. I had a thousand times more confidence in myself. Worries were no longer real, and by removing fear from my life I was able to be successful in my smaller goals. I slowly spiraled upward toward success. Each baby step that I took in attaining success boosted both my motivation and confidence. I was able to open my own Internet business, eventually outsourcing and automatizing most of my work. Passive income was finally mine!

---

[1] Your Brain on Yoga by Sat Bir Khalsa, PhD; with Jodie Gould
http://www.harvardhealthbooks.org/wp-content/uploads/2013/03/YourBrainOnYogaSampleChapter.pdf

Here are some of the most useful tools I have found for practicing meditation on an everyday basis.

Use them in combination at different points in your day. I call it practicing for a reason, not just because you are utilizing the study of meditation, but because you need to actively *practice*. These methods will become easier and easier to use the more often that you do them. The more you use them, the longer a period of time you will be hold the process of meditation, and the stronger you mind will become over what you previously thought had all the power in your life. In reality, you had the controls built in the whole time - congratulations on finally taking the wheel.

1. Guided Breathing Meditations

Guided meditations like this include some sort of person to walk you through them. Thanks to technology, they can be accessed at anytime, anywhere. Listen to them on your phone, iPad, laptop, TV - the list goes on and on. There are video streams online, podcasts, and many other ways you can find them.

You will have to find one that works for you as they are not "one size fits all." Everyone has preference of voice and the style of meditation breathing varies dramatically. I found that I can even find scripts pre-fabricated online and can read and record my own voice.

17

You could also use the voice of a significant other. Your meditation can be personalized for what works best to relax you.

Some may be too distracting for you: too much music, talking, or background noise. The idea is to find a guide that will help you to reach that meditative state. So pick the right guide and they will lead you down a personalized path to peace.

They all generally guide you to concentrate on the breath. You should find a comfortable, quiet place to sit up straight. It is not advised to meditate while driving, when you are about to operate heavy machinery, babysitting - any activity that needs your full attention.

If you have a good memory, you can try practicing a breathing meditation like this one below, but it is not advisable to try and read it while you are meditating.

Breathing Meditation:

A. Find a way to sit upright that is most comfortable for you. Now, with your eyes closed, allow your mind to become quiet. Pay attention to what you are hearing, what your body is doing, what you may be thinking or feeling. Do not delve into those things, just become aware of them. Notice them as if you are an outsider, not a "do-er" of these things. Allow calm to come over you. Do this for a few minutes until you are relaxed.

B. Next, instead of being aware of everything going on inside yourself, observe your breathing. Feel how it passes in and out of your lungs, in and out of your nose all by itself. Do not allow yourself to change it, just let it happen and pay attention to it. Experience how your chest moves up and down, how the rush of air in and out of your body feels, things of that nature.

C. Your brain will drift from paying attention to your breathing to other thoughts. Do not fight it, just wrangle the thought back around and pay attention to breathing. Allow the thought to just pass by you. Let it come in and go out of your mind just as you are breathing. Let all stimuli come and go just as you are breathing.

Do this exercise for as long as you like. Just keep relaxing and bringing your mind back to observing your breathing and its patterns/sensations. The more you do this the easier it will be and the stronger you will become in your mental practices.

I can also recommend this guided meditation which I personally like:

- http://tinyurl.com/GoldingMeditation

19

- Add all of the emotions that you want to feel: relaxation, being very sure of yourself, peace and calm. You feel right at home where you are.
- Be sure to write down all of the people that you would be connecting with. Everyone makes you feel comforted and peaceful. You feel confident in your connections. The littlest details, even how they smile at you, will give you the confidence you need. Everyone makes you feel included and right at home.

For relaxation purposes, I love the beach. It is my favorite place to go and feel calm and peaceful, without a care in the world. It may be a different spot for you, and you can adapt this next exercise to any place that you have experienced extreme relaxation and calm. I have even substituted my experience at the hot springs for the beach. These experiences are full of things that stimulate all of my senses.

A. Picture the beautiful landscape before you. The blue sky, the sparking sand, the blue and white waves crashing in front of you. Seagulls fill the sky. The sun is bright and warm.
B. The sounds of people laughing, waves crashing and the breeze blowing by you fills your ears. The smell of the salt water and suntan lotion fill your nostrils. The warm sand beneath your towel calms you and the bright sun above you beating down on your skin is comforting. The sea breeze cools you off every so often.

C. You walk down to the water, feeling the sand in between your toes after every step. The top layer is dry and warm, and with each step you can feel the cool, moist sand underneath. The cool water from the waves laps at your toes. You inhale the water, it smells so fresh and clean.

D. You lie back down on your towel and close your eyes. The smells, the warmth from the sun, and the sound of the crashing waves lull you into slumber.

Another thing you can add to make these visualizations easier and more realistic would be essential oils. Just pick your favorite smell (for example tangerine, if you want to imagine Christmas with your family, or a cedar tree if you want to imagine yourself in a forest) and put few droplets in your aromatherapy diffuser or oil burner. It will help you relax and bring the presence in the moment. Additionally, it's very healthy. I noticed that nice smells can definitely boost my positive emotions and disrupt the bad ones. You can also use sun lotion (even if it's still winter time) and find some waves/ocean audio on the Internet so it will be much easier to bring all those beach memories back and find serenity. Why not? You can try it. Do whatever works for you.

3. Mindfulness

Mindfulness is a process in which you focus on one thing, while you allow all of your thoughts to come and go naturally. You do not stop them, but you take a step back and basically observe yourself in the now. You put your brain on auto-pilot by focusing your attention to one specific thing while you sit in the passenger's seat for a moment and observe everything going on around you. It takes the focus off of the act of thinking and allows you to take in the moment of now. You are making yourself aware of that very moment and turning your attention away from the past or future, even if only for a few minutes.

It is a difficult process for beginners to learn without a teacher, but it is possible. You can read all about it in books, or in articles on the web. There are many online videos available that will walk you through it. It is called a practice for a reason; it takes practice. Many yoga studios offer mindfulness training as well.

It takes a while to train the brain and get very good at being mindful. It is worth the time it takes though. Research says that even 20 minutes a day is helpful, and that is exactly how I do it, 20 minutes a day, no less. If you think "I don't have time," analyze how much time you spend on time-killers like checking social media, watching TV and other stuff. Mindfulness has been proven helpful for both psychological and physical issues, such as:

- It helps you to enjoy every moment in life as they happen instead of focusing on the past or the future. The past doesn't exist. The future is just a big speculation.

- It will help you to build better relationships of all kinds, as you will not be worrying over things like self-esteem or becoming successful.
- It allows us to relieve stress, which we all know contributes to health problems such as heart disease, pain, high blood pressure, poor sleep patterns, and various stomach issues.
- Therapists have found that mindfulness also is useful in treating those who have depression, anxiety, relationship issues, and problems with abusing dangerous substances.

Mindfulness allows us to accept circumstances and emotions that might otherwise be harmful. By seeing things for what they are, and just being for a moment, it is easier to process things than it is to fight them.

Here is an easy way to start practicing mindfulness right away, even while you are still learning more about it. The more you practice, the stronger the control over your brain will be:

A. First pick a 10-20 minute chunk of time where you can be alone and be comfortable. Find a quiet place. Get rid of anything that will distract you. Yes, turn your phone off (and any other electronic devices too). Just set a timer so that way you do not keep checking how much time is left. I found this helps immensely.

B. You can keep your eyes open or shut them. Many people find that closing their eyes is a plus, but some find it easier to concentrate focusing their vision on an object or by staring straight ahead. I like to focus on a burning candle (fire brings me to the present moment somehow) at home, or on a swinging tree branch when I choose to do it in the forest. Begin taking some long, cleansing deep breaths. Relax, slowly take a look around and after that, visually focus on one object. Then start paying all of your attention/awareness to your breathing. Notice the details. How does it feel as the air is passing through your nostrils, through your esophagus, and into the lungs? Notice your chest rising and falling. Do you have a tingling sensation as the air goes in and the body processes the oxygen? Feel your lungs contracting and expanding with every breath. To start, breathe as deep as you want. At first it will be hard not to change the natural breathing process, but each time you catch yourself doing it, redirect your attention and simply observe what the body does on its own. Do not worry, becoming distracted and redirecting thought to observance is part of the exercise.

C. Each time your mind begins to wander and actively think about a thought or a worry, just bring your attention back to focusing on your breath. You will feel thoughts come and go. This is fine. You want to let them breeze right on through and observe them without thinking about them in the same way that you are allowing the air to pass in and out of your body. <u>Do not think</u>

about not thinking. If you try not to think about something, it's quite obvious you will end up obsessing about it. Just observe and chill out - the "not thinking" part will come eventually.

D. Notice the quiet, the stillness of the moment. The gaps between the mental words. This will relieve stress and help you to appreciate the seconds and minutes that you are currently living. It will help you to actually feel and experience the very moment that you are living, as opposed to the past or the future (a major distraction that keeps us from appreciating the current moments of our lives).

E. Do this for the full 10-20 minutes. You will notice that at first you will be spending most of your time bringing your attention away from thoughts and back to breathing. This is what makes you better at focusing. It is totally normal. The more times that you do it, the easier it will become. When you feel tired of looking at one object or area for so long, just look around slowly. See the sky, notice the ground. If you feel tired of sitting up straight for too long, just slightly change your position. It's okay when you start. Observe and appreciate the beauty around you, all the details, all the smells, all the emotions inside you. Be like a curious little kid.

F. You may also try to focus on one word or phrase. I chose "thank you." I believe that not only is "thank you" one of the most beautiful phrases in the English language, but is also recognized for its deeply healing properties among psychotherapists.

Sometimes I just say "I love you" instead. I say it to myself, but also to everyone and everything in my life. It can really help you stay focused at the very beginning, will bring you good emotions and you may find yourself liking it too much to ever stop. That's fine, too.

I just inhale...

Say "thank you" in my head.

Exhale.

Repeat the process.

G. After some time, you may start feeling a pleasant, warm kind of feeling somewhere between your belly and solar plexus that will give you this lively feeling of a deep presence. It will be caused by the different brainwaves in your brain (alpha or theta, depending on how relaxed and focused you become). If you are consistent in this practice, you may start being able to bring this feeling back very quickly and keep it for a long time, even after you are long done with your mindfulness session - while walking, working, eating or doing anything else in your everyday life. Believe me when I tell you this - words can't even describe how it feels. You will feel alive beyond any description. Alive, present, sober, clear and extremely focused. It took me more than six months to start feeling all these things. Some people never do and it's fine. But even before all these sensations, my life changed in extreme ways, and your life will change as well. Just don't stop. Never stop.

4. Chakra Meditation

There are many different ways to use the chakras in meditation in order to attain physical, emotional and mental well-being. Each chakra is responsible for powering a different area of the physical body, the mind and emotions. They are the proverbial power stations of our life-energy, and it is important to keep them open and in balance to maintain optimum health and wellness.

There are seven major chakras throughout the body. They each have an association point on the body, along with a corresponding color, crystal and element. Chakra means "wheel" in Sanskrit, although they are many times described as a lotus-like flower. Each one rotates or vibrates at a certain speed. When chakras are out of balance, closed, or moving too slowly, one is bound to experience emotional, mental and physical problems because of it. Luckily enough, with practice, chakras can be rebalanced and opened. One of the many ways to do this is through meditation. First though, let me give you a general explanation of each one.

Each has many attributes, including emotion, location, physical processes, and symbols. If you dig even deeper they have many more attributes, including, but not limited to: symbols, oils, musical notes, planets and sounds.

- The Root Chakra (red), is known as the Muldhara. It is located and the bottom of the spinal column, between the genital region and the anal region. Its element is Earth and it moves the slowest of all chakras. It grounds us to the world around us. It is responsible for our survival instincts, our ancestry, and helps us to become self-sufficient and to feel as though we belong. It is responsible for the lower half of the body, including the entire skeleton and teeth, adrenal glands, bladder, circulation of the blood and the spine. All of the other life forces run off of this one, so if it is out of whack or closed, it can cause major dysfunction in the body, mind and spirit.

- Next is the sacral/spleen (orange), which is known as Svadhishthana. It is located near the navel (about two inches or so below). Its element is water and it deals with our sense of taste. It helps us in our relationships (when in balance), is responsible for creativity, sensuality/sexual desires and intuition. It is physically responsible for the sex organs, spleen, gallbladder, urinary system, gonads, intestine (large), the lower back and the appendix. It governs our emotions, especially those related to relationships.

- Above the sacral is the solar plexus (yellow), known as the Manipura. It is located in the upper abdominal area (up to the sternum). Its element is fire and it deals with our sense of sight. It fuels our willpower, ego, how we mentally fuel and process emotion and personality. It is physically responsible for the pancreas, small intestine, stomach, liver, gallbladder, spleen, the middle of the spine, and the nervous system. When in balance, it recharges our spirit.

- Moving on to the heart chakra, called the Anahata (green). It is placed right in the middle of your chest. Its element is air and it deals with our sense of touch. It helps us to feel compassion, have an understanding of others, be nurturing, and to have loving, healthy relationships. It physically governs the heart, lungs, breasts, thymus, shoulders, the hands and the diaphragm. When in balance, it is what fuels unconditional love.

- Following that is the throat chakra, Vishudda (light blue). Its element is sound and it deals with hearing. This chakra is located near our thyroid. It helps us with self-expression and rules communication. It is the chakra that is in tune with the spirit world. Physically it controls the thyroid, bronchial tubes, mouth and trachea. When in balance it helps us to express ourselves positively, without fear of persecution.

- After that is the third eye chakra, Ajna (indigo blue). It is located right between the eyes. Its element is light, and it deals with extrasensory perception. It allows us to have wisdom, internal spiritual guidance, and allows some to have psychic, clairvoyant abilities. Physically speaking, it controls the brain, nose and eyes, nervous system, and pineal gland. When this chakra is in balance, intuition is clearly felt. You also have a better ability to concentrate and your imagination is able to run freely.

- Lastly, we have the crown chakra, Sahasrara (violet). It can be found right at the top of the head. This chakra's element is thought. It is where our awareness is contained. It is also the chakra that controls our intellect and assesses our inner potential. The crown is where meditation is enabled. Physically, it controls the pituitary gland, cerebral cortex and the top of the skull. When in balance, the crown allows us to have an open mind, being completely open to the spiritual realm, and it allows us to transcend.

The more that you practice opening, focusing on, and balancing your chakras, the easier it will become. You will even notice the ability to actually feel them within yourself.

Once I was able to focus on each chakra, I noticed that I had actually felt their presence much earlier in life, before I even knew that they existed.

There are many avenues for practicing chakra meditation, and many ways to learn more about it (books, the internet, yoga, a meditational practitioner, etc.). It is probably easiest to do in guided form at first, but here is an easy exercise that you can put into practice right away. I guarantee that within minutes a day you will notice a difference.

Chakra focus is slightly addicting because you will honestly feel better as a whole (body, mind and spirit). There are so many elements to chakra meditation that it will blow your mind!

A. First I like to ground. To start, shut your eyes. Actively pay attention to your lungs. Feel your breath going in and out. Take a long deep breath. Hold it for three seconds and let it out as slowly as possible.

B. Now repeat this, and this time focus your attention on the ground beneath you. Feel the energy of the earth and your energy connecting to it. Take another breath and let it out. Consciously feel your breath go down your spine and out of your Muldhara (visualize it as a glowing red ball) and into the ground. See in your mind's eye the energy flowing out like roots from your breath, through your chakra, into the ground below you.

C. Now take as many breaths as you need to in order to push out any worry, anxiety, or apprehension that you may be harboring. Use a deep long breath to let these feelings go in the same manner. Take as many as you need until you actually feel grounded.

D. Staying in this position, take seven long breaths. Inhale and exhale deeply and slowly.

E. Imagine again your red root chakra. Feel the warmth of its red light and the energy of it. Keep breathing and as you do, feel breath traveling to this location. Send your breath (you can visualize it as energy or white light) and focus your attention on this chakra. With each breath the light is growing warmer and brighter. Slowly, your red glowing flower is opening. You can feel your life's breath traveling to and from this location (this may take a few minutes and that is fine). Do this until your glowing flower is completely open.

F. Now move through each of the other chakras from the bottom up until each one is open and bright. Take three minutes or so for each one. Allow yourself to fully feel the warm energy in each chakra. You can even pulse the energy up and down through the chakras a few times once they are all open and ignited.

I was a skeptic until I tried it myself. There are so many other exercises involving the chakras. Many you might need to learn from a professional, but I am sure the more you practice, the more you will get from this exercise! I even got a slight energy "buzz" just typing this. I could feel my chakras glowing. Also, bear in mind that you may have an energy rush when it is all over.

There are many more meditational exercises that you can put into practice, both guided and unguided. It is exciting to try new ones.

These are a few easy, everyday tools that worked for me. Have fun weeding out the ones you do not care for and finding new ones that you love!

Your mind will only grow stronger. Your body will find bedtime easier. Your heart and burden will be less heavy and your energy and willpower levels will rise.

At the beginning, the best solution is to focus on just one of the techniques I gave you, just the one you are most fluent with, and you can then proceed further - deepen your knowledge and broaden your spectrum of techniques. Remember: just do one thing at a time.

Even though my favorite means for meditation are mindfulness (which got me started and healed my life) and visual techniques, and I consider myself a down-to-earth person, I found my journey with chakras very enriching and refreshing, so I also encourage you to try it yourself. My friend, a certified massage therapist, aroma therapist and a wellness coach wrote a great practical guide to chakras (the title is "Chakras: Exploring Chakras and Discovering Holistic Wellness - The Practical Approach to Chakras for Personal Development"), which made me start with them in the first place. If you're interested in this topic, I can recommend this book to you without any doubts.

5. Personal Affirmation Meditation

Personal affirmation meditation is another form of guided meditation that involves repeating aloud a set of short phrases and sentences. The text used in this type of meditation aims not only to relax the body and calm the mind, it also promotes healthy self-esteem. The same is true with guided breathing meditations. A prerecorded voiceover will assist you throughout the session, making you restate everything it says. Repeating after the digital voice assistant is important for this technique to become effective. Actually speaking the affirmations aloud helps ingrain positive self-talk into the subconscious. You can even write and record your own personal affirmation script if you want to make it more personal.

I find this meditation technique helpful in making me become more confident and more patient so I can achieve all of the goals I have set for myself. The daily affirmation meditations gave me enough courage and persistence to move toward my targets at a moderate pace, which helped reduce the amount of stress and worry that I used to experience. Furthermore, the regular practice of personal affirmation gradually transformed all negative self-talk in my subconscious into positive self-talk, which gave me wholeness and a brand new sense of worth. It also provided me with a sense of inner calm and peace of mind, with the added bonus of relieving the occasional bouts of headaches and migraines.

Personal affirmation meditation may feel awkward the first time you practice it, and the reason behind it is that we as individuals are typically not used to giving ourselves self-assuring words. It is quite normal to feel uncomfortable or tongue-tied during the first few sessions, but as you continue to do this and you actually begin to feel the positive changes within you, you will slowly get the hang of self-affirmation. As already pointed out, affirming yourself is necessary to boost your inner morale and to experience complete inner healing. In fact, the reason so many people are so insecure and have low self-esteem nowadays is that they haven't praised themselves enough.

There are many ready-made personal affirmation scripts online, but it is also perfectly fine to write your own. If you are more inclined to do the latter, then here are some tips on how to do it.

A. Find a quiet and comfortable place to sit down. Bring a pen and some paper with you. Perform an honest self-examination. Make a list of all the negative and self-depreciating emotions and beliefs you think you have. Beside each negative belief, write down phrases or expressions that refute it. For example, if you think that you always get angry when someone or something interrupts you, refute it with "I am cool and calm whenever interrupted. I welcome the opportunity to know more about the interruption," something like that.

B. Keep in mind that a personal affirmation script does not have to be very long, as you can always repeat the whole thing again if necessary; one page of affirmations is usually enough.

C. Focus more on composing life-giving sentences than trying to fill the page with your script. The content of your script should be free-flowing and uninhibited. When it is sufficient, you will naturally feel it.

D. Carefully check all the self-depreciating thoughts that you think you have and write your script based on them. However, make sure that what you write down is realistic and appropriate, and not to the point of bluffing yourself. You are the only one who really knows what is bothering you, which is why it is important to undergo a careful and honest self-examination.

E. Try using your favorite words, those that make you feel happy, relaxed, content, and confident. This is the beauty of writing your own personal affirmation script; you can use whatever words and phrases you want, and it will never be wrong.

F. After finishing the script, you can now record it. You might even want to put some soothing background music to it, in order to enhance it.

Below are some examples and suggestions of personal affirmation expressions that you can use in your script:

- I am enabled, capable and able.
- I love myself totally and sincerely, without any doubts.

- I love myself first, and that's why I can love others as well.
- I am relaxed and in control.
- I am ready to see the opportunity in changes.
- I am a tower of strength.
- I am formidable under pressure.
- I am positive amidst negative situations.
- I am okay with the past.
- I am okay with the future.
- I am okay with the present.
- I am content with my life.
- I am whole and free.
- I am growing and improving.
- I am perfect as I am.
- I am a blessing and not a burden.
- I bless myself with total serenity.
- I bless myself with peace amidst disarray.
- No matter what happens, I remain cool, calm and collected.

You can also use expressions that are deeply personal to you, like:

- I am capable of earning more money.
- I am very good at saving money.
- I am going to finish the book I am writing.
- I am able to lose weight and reach my ideal weight.
- I am prepared to meet my ideal mate.

These are just some examples of phrases and expressions that you can use for your own script. Be creative and find the right words that speak to you and those that you can better relate to. The same is true with the other meditation techniques. You have to look for something suitable for you.

The Internet contains a vast resource of self-affirmation videos that you can try if you have not created your own yet. Check out these three links below as samples:

- **http://tinyurl.com/confidenceaffirm** – A powerful video that you can use when trying to start practicing personal affirmation meditation.
- **http://tinyurl.com/gratitudeaffirm** – This video is something that you can also use while sleeping. It can help you relieve mental and emotional stresses and wake up feeling wonderful and refreshed.
- Meanwhile, this third video – **http://tinyurl.com/meditbg** – is a 528 Hz sound that can help you boost DNA repair. You can also use it as a background during meditation while chanting your own self-made personal affirmation script.

Keep in mind that with this technique, your spoken voice is of utmost importance. That is why repeating and declaring your script is necessary to make personal affirmation effective. In a way, this method is like infusing positive self-talk into your whole being. Self-talk is a person's inner voice. This inner voice exists only in the mind, in the subconscious, and the goal for applying this method is to direct it, or even alter it if necessary, to make it more positive.

Most of the time, people are not aware of how their self-talk affects their lives negatively. It is a subtle, monotonous commentary going on in the subconscious, and the reason why it is so terrible is that more often than not the comments are negative and self-sabotaging. Personal affirmation meditation crushes this negative self-talk and introduces positive self-talk into the subconscious, boosting the feelings of empowerment and self-worth.

Successful people have learned how to change their negative self-talk into positive self-talk in a consistent manner. Here are some tips on how to properly practice personal affirmation meditation every day:

A. During your first few tries, make it short and do affirmations once a day only. Gradually increase the time spent and the intensity as the weeks go by. As with any other habit, starting slowly allows you to get comfortable without overdoing it. This gradual progression will push you beyond the initial excitement. Five minutes, once a day, is a good start. You can increase your time and the number of sessions per day after every week.

B. Find a nice, quiet place where you can relax and be alone with yourself. It is better to be in a place where you are all alone and there is nothing to interrupt you. For some practitioners, their own bedroom is that ideal quiet space. Others like to do it out in the presence of nature, like at the park or on the beach.

C. Target your negative self-talk. It is necessary to deal with and subdue your negative self-talk before putting in more affirmations. Again, this is the reason why you have to identify your negative self-beliefs while writing your script. When you are aware of how negatively you talk to yourself, you have a better chance of eliminating it. For the first few sessions, concentrate only on refuting this negative self-talk, and then gradually introduce new concepts that you want to develop in yourself.

D. Read your script aloud with emotion and conviction, in order to embed it fully into your subconscious. When you do this daily and repeatedly, eventually your inner critic will turn into your own personal cheerleader.

E. Gradually increase the frequency of your meditations until you can do three sessions a day - morning, noon, and night. The more you do it, the more you get used to it, and the more effective it will become. After the first month, it is possible for you to get used to performing personal affirmation three times a day.

Personal affirmation meditation is a real life-changer, and I am living proof of its effectiveness. It helped me become more confident when facing challenges and untimely crises. It also gave me sufficient motivation and inspiration to finish the things I started, and to reach what I have set out to accomplish. Start practicing this highly useful meditation habit daily and experience the benefits for yourself.

6. Body Relaxation Meditation

Body relaxation meditation is another form of meditation that focuses on the physiological aspect of an individual. Of course, body relaxation techniques also include mental and emotional relaxation, but in general, they are all based on resting and restoring the physical body to take away all its tension and stress.

For an average person, relaxation might mean sitting in front of the TV, eating popcorn or chips, or going to the bar for a couple of drinks to unwind after a stressful day. In fact, I will say that I did some of those things before in order to relieve daily stress; however, I discovered that these things do not do anything to make stress go away, and some of these bad habits could even add to the physical trauma that my body was already experiencing at the time. After doing some research, I found that in order to fight stress effectively, I needed to let my body stir up its own natural relaxation impulses. These natural relaxation impulses can be triggered by staying still, deep breathing, mindfulness exercises, dance exercises and slow repeated movements. If you notice, these triggers are in all the forms of meditation that we have previously discussed.

Body relaxation meditation is actually any form of meditation that puts more emphasis on stimulating these specific natural responses. Regular application of this form of meditation can do a lot to relieve unnecessary stress and to boost overall vitality and disposition.

I keep on saying "unnecessary" stress because your body actually needs some stress for it to stay alive and survive. Stress is also needed when creating or doing something, such as writing, painting, or sculpting; and to a certain extent, stress also helps in studying and learning. It only becomes detrimental to your health when it becomes overwhelming. Lingering stress activates your body's "fight or flight" impulse continuously without rest. This stress impulse exhausts you and drains you of energy. Continuous exposure to this kind of body response is highly dangerous to your general wellbeing.

Natural relaxation impulses are the exact opposite of the "fight or flight" impulses that I just mentioned. They are extremely necessary to stop the continuous stress that you are experiencing every day and they give your body enough time to heal and recuperate.

If you do not allow your body to activate its natural relaxation impulses from time to time, you are in danger of contracting many kinds of chronic health conditions and illnesses.

There are actually a lot of body relaxation techniques that are safe to apply and can effectively stimulate these natural relaxation impulses, and below are some of them.

A. Deep breathing

Deep breathing is the easiest type of body relaxation meditation, and it is also the most essential and most powerful. All of the other techniques are dependent on your mastery of this technique. Deep breathing is the foundation of almost all of the meditation methods that exist today. Nothing is better at providing you with an immediate and readily available sense of relaxation than deep breathing.

Here are some tips on how to practice it properly:

- The most important thing to remember when practicing this technique is to learn to breathe from the belly and not from the chest. That is why it is called deep breathing, because it involves long, deep breaths and not short, shallow ones. When you breathe deeply and from the belly, you breathe in more oxygen, which stimulates your natural relaxation impulses.
- You can apply this technique while sitting, standing or lying down. Make sure that you are as comfortable as possible with whatever position you chose to apply. Place one of your hands on your belly and the other one on your chest to feel the rhythm of your breaths and to act as a guide during the process, which will be explained in detail next.

- The main reason why you should put your hands on your belly and chest is to know if you are applying deep breathing correctly. Proper deep breathing means that you inhale through the nose and exhale out of the mouth. During the whole process, your belly should be the only part that is moving. The chest should stay still or at the very least should only move slightly.
- It is recommended that each inhale and exhale is accompanied by a normal count to four.

B. Progressive muscle relaxation

Although it may sound highly complex and technical, progressive muscle relaxation simply means that you tense up and relax the different muscle groups in your body in a sequential order. It is not that easy to do and may actually take quite a while to get used to, but everything is worth the effort once you get the hang of it. This method is best accompanied by deep breathing techniques for better results.

There are two ways to do this method, and they are *from the face down* or *from the feet up*. Below, you may check out some of the tips on how to execute progressive muscle relaxation.

- Wear baggy clothes and sit or lie down and be as comfortable as possible. It is much better if you are not wearing any footwear or other accessories.

- Begin by performing deep breathing techniques for a few minutes until you are relaxed and ready.

- Depending on which method you chose, start by focusing your awareness on the first body part that you will work on. For the purpose of this example, I will use the *"from the face down* method."

- Focus all of your attention on your face and slowly crunch or wrinkle it as much as you can. Hold it for about 10 seconds then gradually release and relax your face muscles. Remain in this relaxed state for another 10 seconds while still taking deep breaths. Repeat.

- Slowly turn your focus away from your face and onto your neck muscles. Tense your neck muscles for 10 seconds, and then slowly release them, and stay in this completely relaxed state for 10 seconds while taking deep breaths. Repeat.

- Do the same to all the other body parts included in the sequence. For reference, here is the recommended order: face, neck, shoulders, left arm, left hand, right arm, right hand, back, chest, stomach, hips, buttocks, left thigh, right thigh, left calf, right calf, left foot and right foot. For the *"from the feet up"* method, simply reverse the order.

C. Body examination method

This technique is very similar to progressive muscle relaxation, but instead of tightening and releasing your muscles, you fix your attention only on each body part, without actually trying to do anything to the body part. What you need to do is observe the sensation in each part of your body, in a pre-set order, and notice how your current level of fatigue or exhaustion affects them. *From the face down* or *from the feet up* methods are also applicable in this technique. Deep breathing is also incorporated in this method, which can be accompanied by a guided, prefabricated video or audio assistant as well.

- The same as with progressive muscle relaxation, you should wear loose and comfortable clothing, without any footwear or accessories. Sit still or lie down; the important thing is that you must be in a comfortable position.
- Begin with a few minutes of deep breathing.
- Gradually shift your attention to your face. While taking deep breaths, notice all the sensations that you can feel in your face. Notice how each inhale and exhale affects your face. Do this for a few minutes before shifting your focus onto your neck.
- Do the same with your other body parts. Follow the same sequence as you followed in the progressive muscle relaxation technique.

- After you have completed everything, remain in silence for a while, and do some light stretches before ending.

D. Physical exercises such as Yoga, Tai Chi, and Qigong

These physical exercises are more active in nature as compared to the passiveness of the previous techniques, which is why they are more appropriate for people who are seeking physiological stimulation for stress relief.

- Yoga – Widely acknowledged to have originated in India during the 5th or 6th centuries BC, Yoga is an ancient physical, mental and spiritual discipline that involves a wide array of body postures and breath control techniques. Aside from relieving worry and stress, yoga is also effective in developing physical strength, durability, balance and flexibility. Consistent practice promotes the activation of the body's natural relaxation impulses. There are many types of Yoga exercise and some even specifically cater to different groups of people, such as the elderly, pregnant women or people with disabilities.

There are also different forms of Yoga, according to how intense the movements and postures are. The most common are: Satyananda, Kundalini, and Ashtanga. Satyananda, also known as the Gentle Yoga, includes slow movements that are appropriate for beginners. Kundalini is for novice to intermediate practitioners and involves faster, calorie-burning exercises. Lastly, the Ashtanga, also called Power Yoga, is for advanced practitioners who want more intense Yoga workouts that build muscles and promote weight loss. All of these types of Yoga include deep breathing and stretching exercises that induce stress relief. Initially, experts suggest that beginners should have a professional instructor to guide them through the movements and stances until they are adept enough to execute them on their own.

- Tai Chi – Tai Chi is an ancient form of Chinese martial arts that is popular not only for self-defense, but also for the many health benefits it gives to practitioners. Tai Chi's poses promote mindfulness and focus, *chi* (*qi* or life energy) stimulation, and natural relaxation impulse activation. It is indeed another great way to fight off unnecessary stress.

Tai Chi is a low-intensity martial art appropriate for people of all ages and skill levels. Movements are simple and easy to learn, but you can also enroll in instructor-led sessions if you want.

- Qigong – This is another physical exercise from ancient China. Although Qigong is not officially classified as a martial art, it is acknowledged as such by some of its practitioners. In addition to its proven medical benefits, some experts of the craft say that it also has spiritual benefits.

It targets the three core parts of a human being: the body, the soul, and the spirit. The movements of Qigong stimulate and harmonize these three parts, making them work together seamlessly to promote stress relief.

Just as with Yoga and Tai Chi, the techniques and rituals used in Qigong involve slow movements, postures, deep breathing and meditating as well. Beginners will also need the aid of an instructor for more effectiveness.

Aside from relieving stress, Qigong also provides emotional stability and physical strength, it boosts the body's self-healing capacities, and it also develops vascular health.

E. Full body massage

A full body massage is perhaps one of the most common forms of body relaxation that incorporates meditation. Many people are already quite familiar with this method of relieving physical stress and pain. Integrating deep breathing and focusing techniques during a massage session raises the benefits and experience to a higher level.

F. Spa treatment

Like full body massages, a spa treatment is another mainstream or commercialized method of full body relaxation. Actually, some spas provide different kinds of massages as well. There are many different treatments offered in spas, such as aromatherapy, body wrapping, body hair removal, as well as manicures and pedicures. Conventionally, however, the main treatment provided by spas is bathing in mineral-rich water for physical healing. This belief is actually very old and can be traced back to ancient times. As with massages, spa treatments performed by a professional are more effective than trying it yourself at home.

Moreover, you can also incorporate meditation during spa treatments by using deep breathing techniques and focusing on the sensation of each body part that the attendant is currently working on.

You can practice each one, pick just one or only apply a few of your preferences. It is again up to you to pick out those that you are most comfortable with and to discover which ones are more appropriate for your current condition.

Important tip: Your usual reaction to stress can help you discover the best body relaxation technique for you. Consider the following clues:

- Are you temperamental or easily angered when stressed? Then the deep breathing, progressive muscle relaxation and body examination method may be the best techniques for you. These methods allow you to collect your thoughts and live in the moment, thus taking your mind away from the things that trigger your rage.

- Are you exhausted, dispirited or miserable when stressed? If so, then physical exercises such as Yoga, Tai Chi, and Qigong may be the best for you. These rhythmic practices can help lift your spirits and make you feel more alive and in control of your situation.

- Are you physically weak and depleted of energy when stressed? Then a full body massage or a spa treatment is best for you. These two methods alleviate body weaknesses, promote self-healing, and restore vigor and strength.

- Are you an introvert or an extrovert? If you prefer spending some quiet time by yourself, then you should do deep breathing, progressive muscle relaxation, and body examination. If you are more inclined to engage in social activities, then try Yoga, Tai Chi, and Qigong. Full body massages and spa treatments can also be a social activity or a one-on-one engagement.

7. Sitting Positions for Meditation

Sitting is the most common position used for meditation. As mentioned above, you can also meditate while walking, standing up, lying down, or even in the middle of everyday tasks. Just incorporate deep breathing and focusing techniques and you are already meditating. However, sitting is still the preferred position of many advanced practitioners as it is the most balanced and stimulating posture, especially when you are still trying to improve your focus.

There are many types of sitting positions for meditation and I will discuss the most common of them below.

Important tip: Always have some kind of cushion beneath your buttocks whenever you sit for meditation. Since you will be staying still in a single pose for several minutes at a time, it is important that you are comfortable and safe. Without proper padding, your lower extremities, such as your thighs, knees, legs and feet may be injured. Also, whenever you are sitting down cross-legged, always remember to alternate which leg or foot is above and beneath the other, so as to not impair blood circulation. This is actually one of the most common mistakes of newbie meditation practitioners.

A. The regular sitting-on-a-chair position

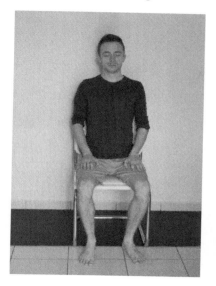 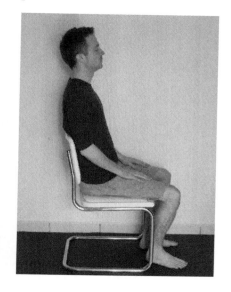

This position is the most basic and most friendly for meditation beginners. For some, it is the most comfortable as it does not stretch any part of the body. The whole body is perfectly relaxed in this posture, without any tension. Sit up straight on a chair. Don't slouch. Place your hands on your lap and align your neck with your back and the whole of your spine. Both of your feet should be touching the ground.

Regular cross-legged position

This is the simplest style of many cross-legged positions in meditation. This style is most suitable for beginners. Sit down and cross your legs in front of you with your feet beneath each knee. Sit straight and make sure that your back is not arched. Rest your hands on your legs, either with the palms facing up or facing the floor.

C. Burmese-style position

In this position, the feet are also in front, but the toes are touching the ground. This is an intermediate posture and requires a bit of flexibility before you can be fully comfortable with it.

D. Siddha-asana position

"Siddha" means enlightened being, and this posture means sitting as an enlightened one. The same procedure as the previous cross-legged positions are used, however, instead of the feet being underneath the knees or their top sides resting on the ground, the right foot is on top of the left foot or vice versa.

E. Half lotus position

Mastering this type of meditation position is a prerequisite before moving on to the full lotus position. Maintaining this posture will require a great amount of flexibility, therefore it will take a lot of practice before it can be done properly. To get into this position, one foot should touch your groin, while the other is on top of it, with the sole facing upward.

F. Full lotus position

As the name implies, this is the complete position of the half lotus with both soles of the feet facing the ceiling. This is an advanced sitting position in meditation, and it requires high level of flexibility. People who have been practicing Yoga or any form of mediation for many years usually use this posture.

G. Seiza position

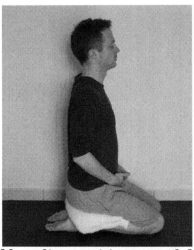

Seiza is also called kneeling position. Kneel down and put a pillow or cushion between your legs and buttocks. The neck and back should be straight. You can also go without the pillow and simply sit on your heels.

8. Unconventional Meditation Techniques

When I was a kid, my grandpa would occasionally ask me to close my eyes and then describe what I was feeling and hearing at that particular time. I noticed that he would make me do this whenever he taught me something practical, like how to tie my shoelaces.

I would follow what my grandpa asked me to do and describe the barking of the neighbors' dogs, the sound of the leaves on the trees moving as the wind blew through them, the gush of water from the nearby stream, and the sound of birds singing in the trees. He would then tell me to continue until I was able to notice everything, even the sound of my own breath. After that, he would tell me to open my eyes and we would then proceed with his lessons. What I did not know then was that my grandfather was actually teaching me the basics of meditation . . .

Because my grandpa knew that I was easily distracted, he would pull me back to the present so my mind would calm down long enough to make it easier to understand his lessons. I didn't know it then, but I was already practicing meditation.

Living in the Moment

The practice of mindfulness is essential in any form of meditation. Most of the stress, disappointments, frustrations, fears and anxieties that we are experiencing at the moment are due to our tendency to dwell in the past or to worry about the future. The truth, however, is that both states - the past and the future - are all an illusion. The only reality is the present. After something happens, it immediately becomes the past; it no longer exists. Meanwhile, the future is yet to happen; it does not exist, or not yet at least. The only thing that exists is the present, so you need to focus on it.

When a person can realize this concept and becomes fully aware of it, their body automatically triggers its natural relaxation impulses, which helps relieve physical, mental and emotional stress.

This goes on to say that meditation can also be performed even when you are not sitting still or in a quiet place of solitude. Below are some unconventional techniques in meditation that you can practice all throughout the day, whenever the opportunity arises.

A. Walking meditation

While walking, fix your awareness on the texture and hardness of the terrain underneath your feet. You can also focus on a single object, such as a tree, a lamp post or a car parked in a driveway. When your mind starts to drift away, gently pull it back again and focus on the ground or your chosen object.

Other opportunities for walking meditation are strolling around your front yard, walking around your neighborhood, taking your dog for a walk, or going on a nature hike. If you don't have enough free time, you can just park your car at the farthest parking spot so you will have a couple of minutes to walk into your office building.

B. Dining meditation

Eating a meal can also be an ideal time to meditate. Not only are you alleviating a lot of stress while eating, you will also have the chance to really savor your meals because you are giving your full attention to it, and in the process you will be eating less. Fix your awareness on the taste of the food or drink. Relish and appreciate each bite and chew slowly. If your mind begins to wander, gently pull it back and notice the texture and flavors of your food.

Take for instance the time when you are drinking your first cup of coffee for the day. To appreciate your drink, completely immerse yourself in the moment; feel the warmth of the cup in in your hands, take note of the smell wafting up to your nose, and notice the slight bitterness that you taste with every sip. If you are not totally immersed in the present you will not even notice that you drank your coffee, which means you did not even get the chance to enjoy drinking it.

C. Driving meditation

This meditation technique should be done carefully. There are only a few moments appropriate for driving meditation, like when you are at a red light, or if you are stuck in gridlocked traffic. Obviously, you must never close your eyes when meditating while driving; just perform deep breathing techniques. When your mind starts to drift away, gently pull it back again to focus on the road and on your breathing. This is very helpful if you are prone to road rage.

D. Idle-time meditation

This type of medication is perfect for when you are in a queue to buy a bus ticket or to pay for groceries, or when you are waiting in a train station, airport or even waiting for a doctor's appointment. You can perform deep breathing techniques or you can just focus on one object near you. You can even do progressive muscle relaxation or body examination method while waiting. Simply notice the sensations in the different parts of your body and follow the suggested sequence.

E. Cardio exercise meditation

You can also meditate while doing cardio exercises like running, cycling or dancing. You can perform deep breathing, focus on a single object or notice your own body parts during your workouts.

F. Daily routine meditation

Lastly, meditation can actually be incorporated in all of your everyday tasks. Make your mundane routines, such as brushing your teeth, washing the dishes, doing laundry, or sweeping the floor, special by fusing meditation techniques with it.

Chapter 3: Meditation and Stillness in Everyday Life

"Why does anxiety, stress and negativity arise? Because you turned
away from the present moment. And why did you do that?
You thought something else was more important.
One small error, one misperception, creates a world of suffering."

–Eckhart Tolle

Worries, stress, things that have not happened yet, they are all not real. The only thing that is real is this very second. Once it has passed, the next second is real. The only way to experience what is real (right now) is to focus on the moment that you are currently experiencing. The best way to do this is through mediation and being still.

Why, you ask? Well, the only way to fully experience the present moment that you are living is to see thoughts, worries and anxiety for what it is . . . from the outside. We have to train our "thinking" and obsessed mind to be still. This does not mean that you will be thoughtless all the time, you will just be able to see exactly what your thoughts are, as an observer.

What is the best way to figure things out, or to see things from an unbiased perspective? Take a step back. Mindfulness and stillness both entail taking a mental "timeout" from active thought. We burn ourselves out every day trying to "think," when in all actuality, not thinking is the way to be less stressed and happy. Thoughts are simply not reality, they are just wasted energy. You will still experience them, you are still aware of them, but you are not actively engaging thinking those thoughts. This will allow you to see them for what they really are - NOT-REAL.

Here in the West, we try to control our emotions. We try to tame them and react differently, we try to change them. But those who truly have found enlightenment, those who know how to live in the "now" and be at peace, have found that it is not about suppressing emotions; it is about seeing emotions for what they are. We have to learn how to detach ourselves from feeling and reacting, and instead view emotions from the outside. The best way to do that is through meditation and taking an ancient Eastern perspective instead.

Deepak Chopra has said this about the Eastern perspective: "This is why Buddha taught that it wasn't important to find out what set your house on fire. It's only important to get out of the burning house as fast as possible." The fastest way possible is to meditate and take a mental "active thinking" break. The best way to be able to separate yourself and get out as quickly as possible is to become mentally strong enough to do so by *practicing* meditation.

Meditation does not have to be stringent exercise. Part of being peaceful and happy is being content in what is happening *right now*. We allow our minds to believe that our thoughts are real, when in reality the only thing that is real is what is occurring this very second. Is anything wrong this very second? No! You *are*, you are being, existing, and nothing is wrong. Too often we perceive that our thoughts are fact, when in reality, in this moment they are not true. The only fact is that in this very moment, everything is as it should be. What happened in the past is not real anymore, and conversely, what we believe may happen in the future is not real either. The only thing you can truly judge as real and true is what is happening this very second.

This is not only a new age, religion-free way of thinking; it is not only a Buddhist or Hindu way either. Even "The Bible" states:

"Finally brethren, whatsoever things are true, whatsoever things are honest, whatsoever things are just, whatsoever things are pure, whatsoever things are lovely, whatsoever things are of good report; if there be any virtue, and if there be any praise, think on these things." *Philippians 4:8 KJV*.

Regardless if you are a spiritual person or not, the idea of focusing on things that are not real (thoughts, worries, fear) is universally known to cause one to not be at peace.

The only way to have power over your emotions is to separate yourself from them. See them for what they are. Emotion is usually triggered by thought. If you choose to actively not think, you will be able to see your thoughts for what they are: fictional.

I was constantly filled with nasty emotions of guilt, fear, worry, and doubt. Until I learned that I was:

70

A) Wasting time (wasting the now, the ONLY thing I truly am and have), the most valuable resource there is, ever was and will be, and

B) Stressing and burning myself out for NO REASON. I was literally TORTURING myself, but I couldn't see that, because I wasn't really there. I was walking through my life in a walking daze. I was a zombie. We don't need all these horror movies, so many people are already zombies these days, and it's even scarier. They really walk around dead.

I had an epiphany one day while bringing myself back to the present moment. I had locked myself in the bathroom at work. I was having a breakdown because I was told that we were going to have layoffs. I was the newest one, so I was sure it would be me. Not to mention, my car payment was a month late and I was living on a friend's couch. I was petrified. I could not even think. I was having heart palpitations. Then, I immediately remembered a video I had been watching on the computer about worry, anxiety, and thought. I looked around. Nothing was actually wrong that very second. Everything I was freaking out about was not real. It was NOT occurring in that very moment. I just saw my scared face in the mirror. But there was no bullet hole in my forehead, no killer behind me. I was okay. It dawned on me that I was wasting the only thing that I had by worrying about things I did not have - that very moment.

I have now figured out that every time I begin to worry, I am throwing away the one thing I do have - my present moment. You do not have to do a mindful meditation to do this. Just sit back, look at your thoughts, look at yourself *right now*, and realize that everything is just as it should be. Otherwise you will toss this very moment into the garbage. You will waste your time, your only ACTUAL presence. Just the act of stopping, looking at right now, realizing you are fine and seeing thoughts for what they are (fake), is a huge act of mindful awareness. It is one of the most helpful things that I have ever realized in my entire life, and is the main way I took my life back.

I found it impossible to achieve almost anything I set out to achieve because of worry, doubt and/or what others might think or say. Focusing on what is happening this very second allowed me to remove the huge rhinoceros of stress I had been lugging around for such a long time. Realizing my current existence, in the current moment, has allowed me to remove the brick wall of fear looming in front of me, paralyzing my actions. By really focusing on the moment at hand, I am free to do as I please. I can achieve anything because my freedom of fear finally allows me to act.

Does that mean you should accept all the jobs you hate, stay away from starting your own business, stay in toxic relationships because "you have to accept what is" and "everything is OK in the now?

Hell no!

The point's being, the ONLY way to change your current situation is in the PRESENT MOMENT.

Wake up and see that - it can't be said enough - there's NOTHING else in this life.

There never was! All the rest is just an illusion.

Just the NOW - the ONLY area where you can act and change anything. When you're constantly beating and torturing yourself like I used to with all these toxic thoughts, emotions, flashbacks and stupid predictions about the future (maybe 0.001% of my black predictions ever came true in my ENTIRE LIFE, but it was quite easy to get rid of these problems, by no means were they fatal or beyond repair, like I used to imagine all the time), there's NO WAY ANYTHING will ever change. You can't even do the proper planning so often, because how can you clearly model your "better future" when you despise this very moment? You can't even really focus and see your current existence as it really is. It's like being a blind pilot in a burning plane.

As one of my favorite bloggers, J. Altucher said:

"You can't buy the happiness using the currency of unhappiness."

Even winning the big lottery wouldn't help much, because you would start obsessing over the future, bad economy, insurance, inflation, investments, protection, bodyguards, war possibilities, your health, your anonymity, *what will your friends think about you and what will people think about you and about the fact that you might make a mistake of some kind and lose all the money, or get robbed or*

KIDNAPPEDFORSOMEKINDOFRANSOM-or-killedbysomerobbers-or-or-or-or-or-or-or-or-and-and-and-and-and-what-if-whatifwhat-if-WHAT IF!!!???...

Uff . . .

Sounds similar? Well . . .

You need to feel good mentally and physically to change ANYTHING, even if for 20 minutes a day. I know how hard it can be. I was heavily depressed too. And then my body started rioting. I spent $3000.00 on doctors, examinations and meds in just the first two days of this mess. And then there was much, much more, a downward spiral.

You need to really start loving your life and yourself.

There's no self-respect and no self-love in punishing yourself with all these thoughts.

Take a deep breath now.

And another one.

Take a look around.

. . .

There's just this very moment.

. . .

This stillness.

The gap between the words, the silence.

. . .

There and there only is all the strength you need.

Only when you start being present and feeling strong, calm and collected can you truly change your life. You can be the conqueror. You can be the big reformer. You can be the positive revolutionist.

I am no longer the "Debbie Downer" that no one wants to be around. I am able to smile freely instead of frowning all the time. I no longer spend my nights thinking, "what if?" My nights are for good sleep or having fun with the people I love. I am able to make the most of my time, and that includes enjoying, in some way, almost every second. Why? That is the only second that matters. It has not only allowed me to be free of anxiety and worry, it has allowed me to find happiness. There is no true peace without realizing that you are fine, right now, this second - you exist.

Now, clearing your head of doubt and worry, stress and fear, you are free to live. Live a healthy lifestyle, not just through diet. It is important to keep your body fit as well as your mind. Exercise regularly and you will find mental and emotion freedom in that as well. Our bodies and our mind work with our essence to make us whole.

I have found that exercising, instead of being inactive and sitting inside having a pity party, is surprisingly a great way to keep my mind in shape, as well as my body. Having an active social life and having relations with others is a great way to feel happy. You will find that the more peaceful and happy you are, the more others will want to be around you. Live your life to the fullest, right now.

You are not your thoughts. You are not your worries. You are not your emotions. You are awake and alive in this very moment - not yesterday, tomorrow or next year. Do not let it pass you by. No one is cheating you, you are only cheating yourself. Do you know this great Radiohead song, "Just?" The chorus goes like this:

"You do it to yourself, you do, and that's what really hurts.

You do it to yourself, just you, you and no one else."

If you are grounded in the present moment, in the reality, no one can hurt you mentally. You are invincible and strong. You cannot be provoked. You cannot be brought to your knees again. You cannot be really afraid of anyone or anything.

You. Just. Are. Can you imagine what this kind of power can do to your life?

Go on. Imagine. Do not let another moment be wasted.

All you have is now, so start now!

. . . Speaking of now, by the end of this chapter, I will have homework for you.

Please, for your own sake, just do it.

First of all, put this book away as soon as you finish reading this chapter and give yourself a gift of 20 minutes of mindfulness or a breathing session. You can use your favorite aroma candles, relax in your favorite chair, sit on your favorite carpet or just go outside and sit on your favorite bench and watch the stars.

Do everything I told you in the previous chapter.

Then, give yourself a gift of this evening, afternoon, morning or whatever it is right now on your part of the planet. Make that time just YOURS.

Forget about your plans. Forget about your deadlines. Just for now.

You are the star of your life and it will be YOUR time now.

Go for a walk to a shop, buy your favorite food, spices and seasonings. The healthier it is, the better you will feel. Your body will reward you. There are so many healthy and delicious things. Go and make a fresh fruit salad with tiny bits of bitter chocolate (it's really great for your brain). Or prepare yourself a delicious vegetable smoothie, squeeze yourself a glass of fresh juice, make an oatmeal with organic honey. Eat some nuts. Cook a crispy, juicy turkey with vegetables. Make a salmon sandwich with wasabi, if you like it spicy.

Whatever. Anything you like.

Celebrate this moment as if you just got a big promotion or your business earned you millions of dollars. Imagine you are about to meet your long-lost best friend. You are that friend. You are about to find yourself again. Celebrate that you are alive, think about all the things you can be grateful for. Turn your favorite music on. Prepare yourself a delicious meal. Grab it, go and watch your favorite movie, TV series, or better yet - read your favorite book. Then make the music louder and dance. Call your friends and tell them how important they are to you and how much you love them. Maybe invite them over if you want. If you feel like it, turn the internet and your phone off. NOTHING will happen.

The world won't collapse, there will be no war because of it, you won't go bankrupt or get sick (on the contrary), I swear!

Lay back, relax, take your time and think about all the things you would really like to do in your life, today and in the near future. Which of these things can you do soon? Do them.

How can you reward yourself for just BEING? Make this time your own holiday. This is the day of NOW, the day of YOU.

From now on, you will start changing everything for the better.

If you feel like sleeping afterwards, just go to sleep. If you want to read your favorite book longer than normal, just do it. Maybe you will feel the urge to take a night walk and just feel the freshness and silence around you. Then do it.

Do whatever pleases you! There's no tomorrow today.

Do this thing at least once a week. Maybe you will have to learn that too, but you have to, and you will. That's the only way out. To start enjoying the present moment and love yourself and your life.

Just because that's the only solution. Just because.

Of course, there's a possibility that you will just feel normal. You just exist. Maybe you don't suffer like I used to. Maybe you just want to relax, see the bigger picture. Do it anyway.

You need it. Everyone does.

Trust me - I was there. I was depressed. Then I was "normal." Then I became quite joyful and now I'm happy. And that's the only wise way to go through this life, the only way to really be successful and to help people around you.

Chapter 4: How to Maintain Inner Peace

Meditation is a practice, something people view as a noun; something that is a belief and an idea; something that is followed. Yet meditation is also something that you need to actively practice: a verb. When there is something that needs to be done, many people need motivation to actually do it.

There is an obvious answer to the question I am often asked, "How do I stay motivated to meditate?" The answer to this, for me, is obvious only because I have been practicing it for some time now. I find the motivation to meditate because I have seen the "proof in the pudding," if you will. The more I meditate, the easier it is for me to:

- Evaluate and separate myself from my emotions. That doesn't mean that I don't feel anything. On the contrary, I can feel much more. All these wonderful feelings that started disappearing as soon as I stopped being a little kid and started "growing up," now I have regained them. But I'm in control of my emotions, not the other way around.

- Achieve my goals, even small steps at a time, whereas before I was paralyzed with fear, unfocused and got nowhere.

- Let go of what other people might think.

- Actually see the beauty and happiness in each moment.

- Concentrate about 500% better and for much longer.

- Really feel what my body wants to tell me. I found my balance and inner peace - I exercise more, take more walks, spend less time in front of my PC, don't overwork myself to death.

- Truly love myself, my life and all the people around me.

- Sleep well, instead of lying awake wondering and worrying.

- Eat better. I healed my bowels.

- Not to be scared of any verbal threats, other people (social confidence) and difficult situations in my life, as well as making complicated decisions.

- Think more strategic and see the bigger picture.

- See all my flaws (so I can work on them), but also my assets.

- Be nice and a self-confident person.

- Be consistent in my actions and plans.

Once you start to see what you can actively do for yourself, you will be motivated to repeat the process. Even bringing your awareness to the very second you are experiencing will allow you to become stronger and better at it. Nothing is more motivating than becoming good at something, especially when that something is peace and happiness. Do not allow yourself to become discouraged when you *do* become stressed out or anxious. It is part of the process, and part of the practice. We are just fragile human beings after all. Look at it as a blessing. You have one more opportunity to strengthen yourself and are one step closer to achieving your goals!

Success is now up to you. You create your life's story mainly with action, not thought. Thoughts are not real - although positive thinking can help you, what you actively do right now is the only reality. There is nothing more motivating than being liberated from anxiety. You can do anything! From here, it is a spiral upward to success!

You must keep going and practicing the meditations. I had a slump a few years back when I did not enjoy anything for a month. I did not want to meditate because I felt "bleh." I had once again allowed myself to be under the power of my thoughts, which of course put me at the mercy of my emotions. I had gone from seeing the beauty and wonder of working in a big city, the magic and marvel in it all, to wondering why I was wandering in a crowd of disgruntled people on the way to work. Why did the corner smell like a bathroom? Why am I surrounded by concrete? When I found myself thinking this way, I realized that my current state of mind had everything to do with my perception of my environment. The city had not changed, the way I viewed it had.

This moment of awakening was a huge motivating factor for me. Practicing meditation allowed me to focus. I had lost my focus. Even the simple act of realizing that I had lost my concentration was an act of redirecting it.

There is nothing better than a reality check to motivate one to meditate. You have notice anytime you start hurting yourself. The onus of my reality was under my control. I had to continue practicing for my own *peace of mind*. Practice does not necessarily make perfect, but it sure makes living life better.

In order to stay motivated in anything, you must figure out why you are doing it. For me, I was doing it because I wanted to change my life in a major way (so called "hard reset") and realized that meditation was a surefire way to bring about radical transformation. I had studied and read a lot about it and knew that this was one thing I had never tried (believe me I had paid for and tried out many different "self-help" options). For you it may be success in a business endeavor, or simply to de-stress because of health issues. Regardless of the reason, you are meditating to improve your life in some way. This should cause you to bump it up on your "to-do list."

Just as you would set aside 30 minutes a day to exercise to get your body healthy, so should you allocate 30 minutes to getting your mind and spirit in shape! Of course you may lose the drive to get up and do it some days, just as someone starting off at the gym might not want to go. The more you do it, the more addicting it becomes.

All in all, staying motivated to meditate starts with one thing: meditation. You do not really have a reason not to try it. You have read the benefits and I have shared with you how it transformed my life, and how it can renovate yours. Like anything else, the first step is to do it. Like I have been saying all along, the only time is NOW! You will not regret it and your motivation will be centered on the results you will see and feel.

Chapter 5: Conclusion

I hope this book was able to help you understand that meditation is for everyone and is useful in every aspect of your life. It is not a club full of yoga masters, monks, hippies and new-agers. It is super practical and universal.

You now know some easy techniques to put into practice each and every day. Mindfulness, guided meditations, visual meditations and chakra meditations are all simply explained. You can easily get started right away! The world of meditation is never boring and there are always new things to try.

The only moment that is real and that matters is right NOW. You understand the importance of now. It is life, it is you, and it is all that counts. Make it count and get started! Life will continue regardless of how we choose to spend it. Because "you reap what you sow."
Do not spend another day stressed, fearful, and discontent. Change is definitely a process, but by starting immediately, you can be living life in a much different fashion in one year.
I am so excited for you. You should be commended for deciding that enough is enough. Here is a pat on the back from me to you. You are one of the few taking the happiness of their lives, and the lives of those around them, into their own hands (or brains rather)!

"Always say "yes" to the present moment. What could be more futile, more insane, than to create inner resistance to what already is? What could be more insane than to oppose life itself, which is now and always now? Surrender to what is. Say "yes" to life - and see how life suddenly starts working for you rather than against you."
-Eckhart Tolle

<u>One last thing before you go – Can I ask you a favor? I need your help!</u> If you like this book, could you please share your experience on Amazon and write an honest review? It will be just one minute for you (I will be happy even with one sentence! Here's the direct link: https://goo.gl/dP9QL2), but a GREAT help for me and definitely a good Karma : -). Since I'm not a well-established author and I don't have powerful people and big publishing companies supporting me, <u>I read every single review and jump around with joy like a little kid every time my readers comment on my books and give me their honest feedback!</u> If I was able to inspire you in any way, please let me know! It will also help me get my books in front of more people looking for new ideas and useful knowledge.

If you did not enjoy the book or had a problem with it, please don't hesitate to contact me at <u>contact@mindfulnessforsuccess.com</u> and tell me how I can improve it to provide more value and more knowledge to my readers. I'm constantly working on my books to make them better and more helpful.

Thank you and good luck! I believe in you and I wish you all the best on your new journey!

Your friend, Ian

Ian

My Free Gift to You

Discover How to Get Rid of Stress & Anxiety and Reach Inner Peace in 20 Days or Less!

To help speed up your personal transformation, I have prepared a special gift for you!

Download my full, 120 page e-book "Mindfulness Based Stress and Anxiety Management Tools" (Value: $9.99) for free.

Moreover, by becoming my subscriber, you will be the first one to get my new books for only $0.99, during their short two day promotional launch. I passionately write about: social dynamics, career, Neuro-Linguistic Programming, goal achieving, positive psychology and philosophy, life hacking, meditation and becoming the most awesome version of yourself. Additionally, once a week I will send you insightful tips and free e-book offers to keep you on track on your journey to becoming the best you!

That's my way of saying "thank you" to my new and established readers and helping you grow. I hate spam and e-mails that come too frequently – you will never receive more than one email a week! Guaranteed.

Just follow this link:

tinyurl.com/mindfulnessgift

Hey there like-minded friends, let's get connected!

Don't hesitate to visit:

-My blog: www.mindfulnessforsuccess.com

-My facebook fanpage:
https://www.facebook.com/mindfulnessforsuccess

-My twitter: https://twitter.com/mindfulness78

Twitter handle: @Mindfulness4Success
-My Instagram profile:
https://instagram.com/mindfulnessforsuccess

I hope to see you there!

Recommended Reading for You

If you are interested in Self-Development, NLP, Psychology, Social Dynamics, PR, Soft Skills and related topics, you might be interested in previewing or downloading my other books:

Paperback version of "Meditation: Beginner's Guide" on Createspace:

http://tinyurl.com/ianmeditationpaperback

Buddhism: Beginner's Guide: Bring Peace and Happiness to Your Everyday Life

Buddhism is one of the most practical and simple belief systems on this planet, and it has greatly helped me on my way to become a better person in every aspect possible. In this book I will show you what happened and how it was.

No matter if you are totally green when it comes to Buddha's teachings or maybe you have already heard something about them—this book will help you systematize your knowledge and will inspire you to learn more and to take steps to make your life positively better!

I invite you to take this beautiful journey into the graceful and meaningful world of Buddhism with me today!

Direct link to Amazon Kindle Store:
https://tinyurl.com/IanBuddhismGuide

Paperback version on Createspace:
http://tinyurl.com/ianbuddhismpaperback

89

Zen: Beginner's Guide: Happy, Peaceful and Focused Lifestyle for Everyone

Contrary to popular belief, Zen is not a discipline reserved for monks practicing Kung Fu. Although there is some truth to this idea, Zen is a practice that is applicable, useful and pragmatic for anyone to study regardless of what religion you follow (or don't follow).

Zen is the practice of studying your subconscious and **seeing your true nature.**

The purpose of this work is to show you how to apply and utilize the teachings and essence of Zen in everyday life in the Western society. I'm not really an "absolute truth seeker" unworldly type of person—I just believe in practical plans and blueprints that actually help in living a better life. Of course I will tell you about the origin of Zen and the traditional ways of practicing it, but I will also show you my side of things, my personal point of view and translation of many Zen truths into a more "contemporary" and practical language.

It is a "modern Zen lifestyle" type of book.

What You Will Read About:

• Where Did Zen Come from? - A short history and explanation of Zen
• What Does Zen Teach? - The major teachings and precepts of Zen
• Various Zen meditation techniques that are applicable and practical for everyone!
• The Benefits of a Zen Lifestyle
• What Zen Buddhism is NOT?
• How to Slow Down and Start Enjoying Your Life
• How to Accept Everything and Lose Nothing
• Why Being Alone Can Be Beneficial
• Why Pleasure Is NOT Happiness
• Six Ways to Practically Let Go
• How to De-clutter Your Life and Live Simply
• "Mindfulness on Steroids"
• How to Take Care of Your Awareness and Focus
• Where to Start and How to Practice Zen as a Regular Person
• And many other interesting concepts...

I invite you to take this journey into the peaceful world of Zen Buddhism with me today!

Direct Buy Link to Amazon Kindle Store:

https://tinyurl.com/IanZenGuide

Paperback version on Createspace:

http://tinyurl.com/ianzenpaperback

Natural Confidence Training: How to Develop Healthy Self-Esteem and Deep Self-Confidence to Be Successful and Become True Friends with Yourself

Lack of self-confidence and problems with unhealthy self-esteem are usually the reason why smart, competent and talented people never achieve a satisfying life, a life that should easily be possible for them.

Think about your childhood.
At the age of four or five, there weren't too many things that you considered impossible, right?
You weren't bothered or held back by any kind of criticism; you stayed indifferent to what other people thought of you. An ugly stain on your sweater, or even worse, on your leggings, was not considered a problem or an obstacle.

You could run on a crowded beach absolutely nude, laughing, go swimming in a city fountain and then play in the sandbox with strawberry ice cream smeared in your hair. Nothing and no one could stop you from saying what you wanted to say, even the silliest things. **There was no shame in your early childhood;** you loved yourself and everyone else.

Can you remember it?
What happened to us?

Parents, teachers, preachers and media **stuffed certain beliefs into your head**, day after day for many years. These beliefs and attitudes **robbed you of your natural, inborn confidence.**
Maybe it was one traumatic experience of some kind that changed you, or maybe it was a slow process that lasted for years. One thing is certain— lacking confidence is not your natural, default state. **It brings you down and now you have to unlearn it.**

Can you name even a single situation in life where high confidence isn't useful?
... Right?

Confidence is not useful only in everyday life and casual situations. Do you really want to fulfill your dreams, or do you just want to keep chatting about them with your friends, until one day you wake up as a grumpy, old, frustrated person?

Big achievements require brave and fearless actions. If you want to act bravely, you need to be confident.
Along with lots of useful, practical exercises, this book will provide you with plenty of new information that will help you understand what confidence problems really come down to. And this is the most important and the saddest part, because most people do not truly recognize the root problem, and that's why they get poor results.

In this book you will read about:
-How, when and why society robs us all of natural confidence and healthy self-esteem.
-What kind of social and psychological traps you need to avoid to feel much calmer, happier and more confident.
-What "natural confidence" means and how it becomes natural.
-What "self-confidence" really is and what it definitely isn't (as opposed to what most people think!).
-How your mind hurts you when it really just wants to help you, and how to stop the process.
-What different kinds of fear we feel, where they come from and how to defeat them.
-How to have a great relationship with yourself.
-What beliefs and habits you should have and cultivate to succeed.
-How to use stress to boost your inner strength.
-Effective and ineffective ways of building healthy self-esteem.

-How mindfulness and meditation help boost, cultivate and maintain your natural confidence.
-Why the relation between self-acceptance and stress is so crucial.
-How to stay confident in professional situations.
-How to protect your self-esteem when life brings you down and how to deal with criticism and jealousy.
-How to use neuro-linguistic programming, imagination, visualizations, diary entries and your five senses to re-program your subconscious and get rid of "mental viruses" and detrimental beliefs that actively destroy your natural confidence and healthy self-esteem.

In the last part of the book you will find 15 of the most effective, proven and field-tested strategies and exercises that help people transform their lives.

Take the right action and start changing your life for the better today!

Direct Buy Link to Amazon Kindle Store:
https://tinyurl.com/IanConfidenceTraining

https://tinyurl.com/IanConfidencePaperback

Do you believe your life would be healthier, happier and even better, if you had more practical strategies to regulate your own emotions?
Most people agree with that.

Or, more importantly:

Do you believe you'd be healthier and happier if everyone who you live with had the strategies to regulate their emotions?

...Right?

The truth is not too many people actually realize what EQ is really all about and what causes its popularity to grow constantly.

Scientific research conducted by many American and European universities prove that the **"common" intelligence responses account for less than 20% of our life achievements and successes, while the other over 80% depends on emotional intelligence.** To put it roughly: **either you are emotionally intelligent, or you're doomed to mediocrity, at best.**

As opposed to the popular image, emotionally intelligent people are not the ones who react impulsively and spontaneously, or who act lively and fiery in all types of social environments.

Emotionally intelligent people are open to new experiences, can show feelings adequate to the situation, either good or bad, and find it easy to socialize with other people and establish new contacts. They handle stress well, say "no" easily, realistically assess the achievements of themselves or others and are not afraid of constructive criticism and taking calculated risks. **They are the people of success.** Unfortunately, this perfect model of an emotionally intelligent person is extremely rare in our modern times.
Sadly, nowadays, **the amount of emotional problems in the world is increasing at an alarming rate.** We are getting richer, but less and

less happy. Depression, suicide, relationship breakdowns, loneliness of choice, fear of closeness, addictions—this is clear evidence that we are getting increasingly worse when it comes to dealing with our emotions.

Emotional intelligence is a SKILL, and can be learned through constant practice and training, just like riding a bike or swimming!

This book is stuffed with lots of effective exercises, helpful info and practical ideas.

Every chapter covers different areas of emotional intelligence and shows you, **step by step**, what exactly you can do to **develop your EQ** and become the **better version of yourself**.

I will show you how freeing yourself from the domination of left-sided brain thinking can contribute to your inner transformation—**the emotional revolution that will help you redefine who you are and what you really want from life!**

In This Book I'll Show You:

- What Is Emotional Intelligence and What Does EQ Consist of?
- How to **Observe and Express** Your Emotions
- How to **Release Negative Emotions** and **Empower the Positive Ones**
- How to Deal with Your **Internal Dialogues**
- How to **Deal with the Past**
- **How to Forgive** Yourself and How to Forgive Others
- How to Free Yourself from **Other People's Opinions and Judgments**
- What Are "Submodalities" and How Exactly You Can Use Them to **Empower Yourself** and **Get Rid of Stress**
- The Nine Things You Need to **Stop Doing to Yourself**
- How to Examine Your Thoughts
- **Internal Conflicts** Troubleshooting Technique
- The Lost Art of Asking Yourself the Right Questions and **Discovering Your True Self!**
- How to Create Rich Visualizations

• LOTS of practical exercises from the mighty arsenal of psychology, family therapy, NLP etc.
• **And many, many more!**

Direct Buy Link to Amazon Kindle Store: https://tinyurl.com/IanEQTrainingKindle

Paperback version on Createspace: https://tinyurl.com/ianEQpaperback

Communication Skills Training: A Practical Guide to Improving Your Social Intelligence, Presentation, Persuasion and Public Speaking

Do You Know How To Communicate With People Effectively, Avoid Conflicts and Get What You Want From Life?

...It's not only about what you say, but also about WHEN, WHY and HOW you say it.

Do The Things You Usually Say Help You, Or Maybe Hold You Back?

Have you ever considered **how many times you intuitively felt that maybe you lost something important or crucial, simply because you unwittingly said or did something, which put somebody off?** Maybe it was a misfortunate word, bad formulation, inappropriate joke, forgotten name, huge misinterpretation, awkward conversation or a strange tone of your voice?
Maybe you assumed that you knew exactly what a particular concept meant for another person and you stopped asking questions?
Maybe you could not listen carefully or could not stay silent for a moment? **How many times have you wanted to achieve something, negotiate better terms, or ask for a promotion and**

failed miserably?

It's time to put that to an end with the help of this book.

<u>**Lack of communication skills is exactly what ruins most peoples' lives.**</u>
If you don't know how to communicate properly, you are going to have problems both in your intimate and family relationships.

You are going to be ineffective in work and business situations. It's going to be troublesome managing employees or getting what you want from your boss or your clients on a daily basis. Overall, **effective communication is like an engine oil which makes your life run smoothly, getting you wherever you want to be.** There are very few areas in life in which you can succeed in the long run without this crucial skill.

What Will You Learn With This Book?

-What Are The **Most Common Communication Obstacles** Between People And How To Avoid Them
-How To Express Anger And Avoid Conflicts
-What Are **The Most 8 Important Questions You Should Ask Yourself** If You Want To Be An Effective Communicator?
-**5 Most Basic and Crucial** Conversational Fixes
-How To Deal With Difficult and Toxic People
-Phrases to **Purge from Your Dictionary** (And What to Substitute Them With)
-The Subtle Art of **Giving and Receiving Feedback**
-Rapport, the **Art of Excellent Communication**
-How to Use Metaphors to **Communicate Better** And **Connect With People**
-What Metaprograms and Meta Models Are and How Exactly To Make Use of Them To **Become A Polished Communicator**
-How To Read Faces and **How to Effectively Predict Future Behaviors**
-How to Finally Start **Remembering Names**
-How to Have a Great Public Presentation
-How To Create Your Own **Unique Personality** in Business (and Everyday Life)
-Effective Networking

Direct link to Amazon Kindle Store:
https://tinyurl.com/IanCommSkillsKindle

Paperback version on Createspace:
http://tinyurl.com/iancommunicationpaperback

Speed Reading: How to Read 3-5 Times Faster and Become an Effective Learner

No matter if your objective is to **do great during your university exams**, become a **bestselling writer** or start **your own business,** you will have to read A LOT, and I mean it. Reading takes time. **Time is our most valuable asset**—nothing new here.

You can always make money or meet new friends, but **you will never be able to "make time."** The only way to succeed and have a happy life without regrets is to use it wisely and **learn how to manage and save it.**

In this book, I will take you through the dynamics of speed reading in a way you may have never imagined before. I'm here to preach the need for speed reading and make use of some of the principles that can steer your knowledge and productivity in the right direction.

Learn How to Read 5 Times Faster, Remember Much More and Save Massive Time!

In This Book You Will Read About:
• The History of Speed Reading

- Popular Speed Reading Myths
- **Environment and Preparation**
- How to Measure Your Reading Speed
- **Key Speed Reading Techniques**
- Reading Tips for Computer and Tablet
- Common Reading Mistakes to Avoid
- Easy and Effective Memory/Learning Techniques
- **Dealing with Tests and Diagrams**
- **Practical Exercises and Eye Adjustments**
- Useful Links and Ideas
- Diet
- How to Track Your Progress
- Proper Motivation and Mindset

Direct Buy Link to Amazon Kindle Store:
https://tinyurl.com/IanSpeedReading

Paperback version on Createspace:

http://tinyurl.com/ianreadingpaperback

About The Author

Author's Blog: www.mindfulnessforsuccess.com

Amazon Author Page: http://www.amazon.com/author/iantuhovsky/

Hi! I'm Ian...

. . . and I am interested in life. I am in the study of having an awesome and passionate life, which I believe is within the reach of practically everyone. I'm not a mentor or a guru. I'm just a guy who always knew there was more than we are told. I managed to turn my life around from way below my expectations to a really satisfying one, and now I want to share this fascinating journey with you so that you can do it, too.

I was born and raised somewhere in Eastern Europe, where Polar Bears eat people on the streets, we munch on snow instead of ice cream and there's only vodka instead of tap water, but since I make a living out of several different businesses, I move to a new country every couple of months. I also work as an HR consultant for various European companies.

I love self-development, traveling, recording music and providing value by helping others. I passionately read and write about social psychology, sociology, NLP, meditation, mindfulness, eastern philosophy, emotional intelligence, time management, communication skills and all of the topics related to conscious self-development and being the most awesome version of yourself. Breathe. Relax. Feel that you're alive and smile. And never hesitate to contact me!

Printed in Great Britain
by Amazon